D1560168

THE
WEDGE–GAME
POCKET
COMPANION

THE
WEDGE–GAME
POCKET
COMPANION

JIM MCLEAN and
JOHN ANDRISANI

HarperCollins*Publishers*

HarperCollins books may be purchased for educational, business, or sales promotional use. For information, please write: Special Markets Department, HarperCollins Publishers, Inc., 10 East 53rd Street, New York, NY 10022.

Library of Congress Cataloging-in-Publication Data
McLean, Jim.
    The wedge-game pocket companion/by Jim McLean and John Andrisani.—1st ed.
        p. cm.
    ISBN 0-06-270141-X
    (flexbind: alk. paper)
    1. Wedge shot (Golf). I. Andrisani, John. II. Title.
GV979.W43M35 1995
796.352'34—dc20   95-23231
95 96 97 98 99 ❖ / HR 10 9 8 7 6 5 4 3

CONTENTS

FOREWORD

Since pitch shots, sand shots, and chips, played with either the pitching wedge, lofted wedge, or sand wedge, make up the guts of the game of golf, I'm excited to present amateur golfers with *The Wedge-Game Pocket Companion*.

Because I'm the senior editor of instruction at *GOLF Magazine,* I've had the opportunity to work with more than one hundred PGA Tour professionals, many of whom—most notably, Chi Chi Rodriguez—possess superb touch.

I've also had the opportunity to play with some big-name pros, including Seve Ballesteros, who, according to the savviest golf aficionados, is still the game's most talented wedge player.

The lessons I've learned from Chi Chi and Seve, plus other professionals known for their finesse around the green, are reflected in this book. Also included are those shots I've learned through trial and error over 38 years of playing this great game on courses around the world.

Happily, Jim McLean, the co-author of *The Wedge-Game Pocket Companion* and one of golf's most outstanding instructors, will also teach you an array of shots that he's learned from years of experience.

With this arsenal of wedge shots in your bag, you no longer have an excuse for not going out and lowering your handicap.

-John Andrisani

INTRODUCTION

Perhaps the greatest concept in modern golf was the ingenious invention of the sand wedge by Gene Sarazen, in 1932.

I played with Mr. Sarazen six or seven times when I worked one winter at Marco Island in Naples, Florida. It was quite a thrill to tee it up with one of the all-time great golfers, and visit with him and hear some of the history behind his invention.

According to Sarazen, he was learning to fly during the winter of 1931 when he noticed that lowering an airplane's tail flaps made the nose rise. He figured that same principle could apply to clubmaking: Lower the tail of the club below its leading edge, to help it slide through the sand and lift the ball up into the air.

Shortly after his flying lesson, "The Squire" experimented by applying solder to the back of standard niblick clubs, filing them down, adding more solder, then finally testing the results in a bunker on the golf course of his Florida home.

Six months later, Sarazen had a club that helped him recover from sand much more easily than ever before. He also used it to hit a variety of greenside shots. The wedge worked so well that Sarazen took it with him to the 1932 British Open; he won that coveted championship because of the wonderful shots he played with the wedge.

Wilson introduced Sarazen's "R99" sand wedge in 1934, and the average golfer, as well as the club pro, had a new weapon to battle the course with.

Along with the sand wedge, nowadays many golfers carry a pitching wedge and a lofted wedge in their bags. And why not? The wedges are the chief scoring clubs. They are the clubs that can help you set up a birdie on a short par-4 hole or a long par-

5 hole. More important, they can help you salvage par when your approach shots (or tee shots on par-3 holes) go astray. For this reason, I'm going to tell you all I know about wedge play, based on what I've learned through my own experience and from talking, and playing with, the game's most talented teachers and PGA professionals.

What I've learned from being around such masters as Claude Harmon Sr., Johnny Revolta, Ken Venturi, and Paul Runyan I pass on to both amateur and pro students practically every day. Now it's your turn to learn these vital tips on wedge play from me and my co-writer, John Andrisani.

Andrisani, who is the senior editor of instruction at *GOLF Magazine,* has written numerous articles and books with many modern-day great players, who have described to him in detail how they play specialty shots with the wedges. Therefore, it goes without saying that he has some shot-making gems of his own to share with you.

All 100 tips in *The Wedge-Game Pocket Companion* are purposely brief and concise. We do not kill you with detail. These tips are solid, and should help you improve some part of your wedge game.

I sincerely hope reading this book brings you enjoyment, a newfound appreciation for wedge shots, and lower scores!

-Jim McLean

CHAPTER 1

THE PITCHING GAME

HOW TO PITCH OFF HARDPAN

Many club-level golfers panic unnecessarily when they find their ball lying on firm ground, called "hardpan." In fact, it can be easy to hit a solid pitch off this lie. The secret to hitting a good recovery shot is setting up correctly.

At address, play the ball back in your stance, with your hands ahead of it. Put 70 percent of your weight on your left foot.

This address position encourages you to make a steeper backswing than normal, then hit sharply down into the ball.

Hitting off hardpan is easy, provided you assume this type of setup.

HOW TO RECOVER
FROM A DIVOT

The critical link to hitting a solid pitch shot from a divot in the fairway is to stay down through impact while your hands lead the club into the ball.

Keeping your head down a split second longer will help you accomplish that goal.

*To recover from a divot, be sure your hands
lead the clubhead on the downswing.*

ANTIFREEZE

Those of you who freeze over the ball for several seconds, then yank the club back violently along an exaggerated inside path, should try using a slight "forward press" to trigger a smooth swing.

Press your hands a tad toward the target, or press your right knee inward. A split second later, start your swing.

*Use a forward press to help you trigger a
smooth swinging action.*

PLAY THE PITCH–AND–RUN "ADVANCE SHOT"

When the entrance to a green is unguarded by bunkers, the pin is back, and your ball is on fairway grass around 30 to 40 yards from the hole, play a pitch-and-run shot with a pitching wedge.

Assume a "closed" stance by setting up with your right foot farther from the target line than your left foot.

Swing the club back on a shallow arc.

Coming down, concentrate on rotating your right arm over your left. That way, the toe of the clubhead will lead its heel, putting a slight degree of hook spin on the ball.

This shot will come in hot, skid, then run to the hole that's situated at the back of the green.

In playing the pitch-and-run, swing the club back on a shallow arc.

HIGH PITCH

To hit an extra-high pitch over a tree that stands between you and the hole, play the ball forward in your stance, with your hands behind it. Grip the club lightly to promote supersoft wrist action.

Keep your head steady on the backswing.

Keep your head behind the ball through impact, and concentrate on swinging your arms into a high finish position.

A forward ball position is critical to hitting a high pitch shot.

THE SECRET TO SLOWING DOWN YOUR FAST SWING

The majority of club-level golfers swing too fast on wedge shots because they exaggerate hand action in the takeaway.

If this is your problem, practice hitting pitches with your feet together. This drill teaches you to swing more with your arms than your hands, so that your action slows down automatically.

This feet-together drill will quickly train you to make a slower swing.

HOW TO STOP
HITTING A PUSH

If, on pitch shots, you tend to push the ball well right of target, try setting your feet, knees, hips, and shoulders slightly left of the target line.

This open setup position allows you to swing your arms more freely on the downswing, and square the clubface to the ball at impact.

TAILORING THE TIP: In order to groove the right swinging action, put a glove under your left armpit; then make sure to keep it from falling out as you employ a short follow-through.

Assume an open setup position to promote a connected swing and square contact with the ball.

THE WIND-CHEATER

To hit an extra-low, boring pitch shot that cheats the wind, play the ball toward the back of your stance and set your hands a couple of inches ahead of it. Also, put between 60 and 70 percent of your weight on your left foot.

Take the club up abruptly on the backswing. Narrow and steep! Actually feel your hands go "up" on the backswing.

On the downswing, keep the follow-through short and your left wrist rock solid.

When playing a wind-cheater, set your hands well ahead of the ball.

HOW TO CURE A PULL

If, on pitch shots, you tend to pull the ball left, you're probably coming over the shot with your right side.

Set your body square to the target line, so that imaginary lines running across your feet, knees, hips, and shoulders are parallel to another imaginary line running from the ball to the target.

Now, focus on a slight inside loop. Concentrate on hitting the inside quadrant of the golf ball. Finally, feel a little extra pressure in the last three fingers of the left hand. This will help you lead the club down, keep a solid left wrist position, and keep the clubface square at impact.

Assuming a square setup is one key to preventing the wicked pull shot.

HOW TO STOP
HITTING FAT SHOTS

The reason so many amateur golfers hit "fat" pitch shots, meaning the ball flies only a very short distance, landing well shy of the hole, is because they let their left arm bend severely on the backswing. This fault usually causes you to exaggerate your wrist's hinge action at the top of the swing, then "throw" the club down sharply, into the turf behind the ball.

To remedy this problem, swing back keeping your left arm straight but not tense. Maintain the straight left arm position on the downswing, so that you feel your left side pull the club through the ball.

Keeping your arm straight can stop you from hitting fat pitch shots.

BACKYARD PRACTICE

To learn how to judge distance and enhance your touch on short pitch shots with the lofted wedge, set a dozen balls down on your backyard lawn, about five yards away from a water bucket (or basket).

Try to hit each shot into the bucket.

Gather up the balls, then move the bucket to another spot on the lawn, 10 yards away.

Finally, practice hitting 15-yard pitches. This sort of focused practice will make you ready for the challenge of pitching the ball close to the cup on the course.

*Practice hitting
balls into a water
bucket to enhance
your touch.*

HOW TO CURVE THE BALL
FROM RIGHT TO LEFT

To hit pitch shots that curve left in the air, then spin farther left after landing on the green, aim your body to the right (where you want the ball to start its flight) and the clubface dead square to the flag (where you want the ball to land).

Swing normally.

The more you want the ball to curve left, the farther right you should aim your body, and the more you should close the clubface.

This unique setup will enable you to curve the ball to the left.

HOW TO CURVE THE BALL FROM LEFT TO RIGHT

To hit pitch shots that curve right in the air, then spin farther right after landing on the green, aim your body to the left (where you want the ball to start its flight) and the clubface slightly open to the flag (where you want the ball to land).

Swing normally.

The more you want the ball to curve right, the farther left you should aim your body.

This unique setup will enable you to curve the ball to the right.

If your direction is off when playing pitch shots, you're probably not aligning your clubface squarely to the target at address.

A good way to correct this problem is to set the club square to an "interim target" (leaf, bare spot, etc.) located along the target line and only a couple of yards in front of you. Line the leading edge of your wedge directly at the interim target.

Use an interim target to help you set the club down in a square position.

SHORT AND SWEET

To hit a mini, 20-yard pitch from a grassy greenside lie, first select a sand wedge.

Next, square the clubface to your target.

Then make a short, very controlled backswing action.

Employ a brisk forward swing, making sure to hit the ball before taking a divot. Do not allow the clubface to turn over through impact. Employ a short, firm finish.

The ball will be lifted out of the grass, float nicely in the air, then land softly on the green.

To pop the ball out of a grassy lie, make a brisk swing and keep the finish short.

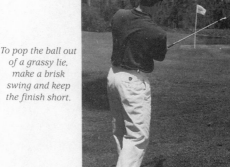

Whenever you need to hit a superhigh, supersoft, supershort shot with a sand wedge, use the following technique used by Seve Ballesteros:

Choke down on the grip.

Stand as far away from the ball as is comfortably possible with your feet in an open position.

Lower your hands dramatically.

Set the clubface wide open.

On the backswing, set the club in an even more open position.

Swing down, trying to point the knuckles of your left hand skyward. This will help you slide the clubface underneath the ball and hit it superhigh.

Choking down on the club is a key to hitting Seve's super-soft pitch.

PUT YOUR RIGHT HAND IN "NEUTRAL"

If a friend or playing partner confirms that your clubface and body alignment are correct, but your pitch shots drift off to the right of the green, your right hand grip is probably too weak.

Assuming a neutral right-hand grip will solve your direction problem once and for all.

To check that you've correctly assumed a neutral right-hand grip, look down and see that the V formed by the thumb and forefinger of that hand points between your chin and right shoulder.

This neutral right-hand grip will help you hit more accurate pitch shots.

TURN, TURN, TURN

If you're not hitting the ball as far as you think you should with your 60-degree lofted wedge, turn the toe end of your right foot out about 30 degrees.

This setup adjustment will promote a fuller turn of the body and, in turn, more clubhead speed and distance.

Turn your right foot out to promote a fuller turn and stronger shots.

One shot that causes the average golfer anxiety is the short pitch from the fairway.

Because you probably don't hit the ball far enough to reach par-4 holes in two shots, or par-5 holes in three shots, you often face this shot, too.

The short pitch does not require a full swing, but rather depends a lot on feel. So practice hitting to targets in the 40-to-60-yard range. Make sure to pace off these yardages, so that you'll feel comfortable you can pitch the ball precise distances and to tight pin locations.

Hit to "short targets" to groove a good feel for playing pitch shots.

DON'T LET YOUR
LEFT WRIST BEND

Another way to promote on-line pitch shots is to follow this advice when you're in the hitting area:

Keep the back of your left wrist virtually flat and practically in line with the clubface's leading edge. Maintaining your grip pressure will help you accomplish that goal.

The next time you're practicing pitch shots, hold your short finish position, then check your left wrist position.

Concentrate on a firm left wrist position to enhance your direction control.

THE CUT SHOT

One thing top pros have in common is the ability to hit a soft cut shot over a bunker to a tight pin. Here's how to loft the ball out of rough, so that it has soft flight and stops quickly on the green.

Play the ball forward in an open stance.

Open the clubface of a sand wedge.

Swing the club back outside the target line.

Swing across the ball coming through, so you impart "cut spin" on the ball.

Swing the club back outside the target line when playing a cut shot.

YES, YOU CAN RECOVER FROM WATER

When the ball is in water near the green, don't automatically take a drop and a one-shot penalty stroke.

You can hit a good recovery shot, provided at least half of the ball is above the water's surface and you can take a relatively firm stance. Use the following technique.

When addressing the ball, open the face of your sand wedge only slightly.

Swing the club back on an upright plane.

Swing down on a sharp angle, so the club contacts the water close behind the ball.

When playing from water, open the face of your sand wedge, then hit the shot as you would from a bunker.

LOOKS CAN BE DECEIVING

A lie that looks easy but can give you trouble if you're not careful is when the ball is perched up high in rough.

In fact, when playing a short pitch from this type of lie, many golfers tend to take a club that's too lofted and hit the ball short of the hole. That's because the soft grass under the ball allows them to hit up on the ball more easily.

To guard against this, take a pitching wedge instead of a sand wedge or third wedge, and make a three-quarter swing.

One more thing: Be careful not to ground the club, because the ball could easily drop into a much worse lie.

Off a perched lie, use less club and a three-quarter swing.

THE LOW-BURNER

Yes, you can hit a sand wedge shot that flies low, bounces three or four times on the green, checks up, then rolls to the pin. Here's how:

Play the ball well back in your stance. Set your hands opposite the middle of your left thigh, so that you automatically lean the shaft well forward. Set the leading edge of the clubface square to the target.

From this setup, make a firm, relatively brisk backswing.

On the downswing, keep the finish low and very short.

Lean the shaft toward the target when setting up for the low-burner.

STOP IT!

In preparing to hit a low, quick-stopping pitch shot from the 20-to-40-yard range, remind yourself to finish with the clubshaft pointing at the target.

This preswing key will encourage you to keep the clubhead low to the ground in the hitting area, keep the clubface on the ball a split second longer, and finish low.

When hitting a "stop shot," the clubshaft should finish up pointing at the target.

WHAT TO DO
WHEN PITCHING OFF
AN UPHILL LIE

When playing a pitch off an uphill lie, set up with your body tilted to your right, so that you stand perpendicular to the slope. By addressing the ball in this manner, in effect you give yourself a flat lie.

Once you're set up, just make your normal swing and the club's arc will follow the slope.

Tilt your body to your right when playing a pitch off an uphill lie.

HIGH, HIGH, HIGHER

When hitting an extra-high pitch shot, it's important that you complete the finish. You can't just hit the ball and stop.

To promote the correct action, think of finishing with the club-shaft pointing at the sky.

To promote an extra-high shot, try to finish with the clubshaft pointing at the sky.

THANKS, KEN

Here's how to play a soft landing pitch shot that Ken Venturi played a lot from tight lies during his heyday.

Assume your normal pitching address, but stand farther from the ball than normal, with the shaft straight up and down (not leaning toward the target).

Swing back normally.

Coming down, try to return the clubshaft to its starting position; this downswing key will encourage you to employ a super-firm hit-and-hold impact position, and stop you from closing the clubface.

A straight shaft position is critical to playing Venturi's soft pitch shot.

WHAT TO DO WHEN PITCHING OFF A DOWN-HILL LIE IN THE FAIRWAY

When playing a full pitch shot off a downhill lie, always play the ball closer to your back foot. This setup position will enable you to make more solid contact with the ball.

Mimic this setup position to hit solid pitch shots off downhill lies.

WHAT TO DO WHEN
PLAYING A VERY SHORT
GREENSIDE PITCH OFF A
DOWNHILL LIE

WHAT TO DO WHEN PLAYING A VERY SHORT GREENSIDE PITCH OFF A DOWNHILL LIE

When your ball is on a downhill slope by the green and you have to lift the ball up quickly—and stop it quickly, too—this technique will save you.

With the ball played back in a very open stance, set your hands even with your back leg.

Going back, swing the club up abruptly.

On the downswing, slice across the ball, using a "chop" stroke.

Assume this setup when playing a short pitch off a downhill lie.

THE LOB SHOT

In playing the lob shot from near the green, cock your wrists early in the backswing while keeping your head steady.

On the downswing, uncock your wrists and strive for a full finish. Allow your wrists to re-cock in the follow-through.

This action will ensure that the ball stops dead as soon as it hits the green.

When playing a lob shot, cock your wrists
early in the backswing.

WHAT TO DO WHEN THE
BALL IS ABOVE YOUR F

On a hilly course, when the ball is above your feet, the tendency is to swing on an exaggerated flat plane. Consequently, the shot will fly from right to left.

To compensate for this flight pattern, aim the clubface slightly right of the target.

*When the ball is above your feet,
aim right of target.*

WHAT TO DO WHEN THE BALL IS BELOW YOUR FEET

When the ball is below your feet, the shot will fly to the right of target. Allow for this flight patttern by aiming the clubface to the left of target when taking your address.

When the ball is below your feet, aim the clubface left of target.

CHAPTER 2

SAND–PLAY SAVVY

COPY SEVE

If you face a short sand shot, over a high lip, to a tight pin, do what Seve Ballesteros does:

Choke down on the club, so that your right hand holds the steel shaft.

This grip encourages you to swing the club on a very upright plane and slide the club under the ball more easily.

Choking down helps you slide the club into the sand, then under the ball.

FIRST, REHEARSE YOU[R]
FOLLOW-THROUGH

To promote good clubhead acceleration when pl[aying a] normal explosion shot from sand, imagine yourself s[winging] into a follow-through position before you swing.

Mimic that visual image when you actually swing.

To hit good sand shots, visualize yourself
following through before you swing.

NO POT LUCK

Many modern courses feature pot bunkers, very similar to those on the course of St. Andrews, in Scotland.

Should you ever find your ball in the middle of one of these greenside hazards and you face a delicate shot, set the club down with the face wide open, make a very wristy upright backswing, and use your right hand to slap the sand with the bottom of the club.

Lay the face wide open when playing a sand shot from a deep pot bunker.

WHAT TO DO WHEN THE BALL SITS PARTIALLY IN SAND, PARTIALLY IN GRASS

Sometimes the ball will sit on the edge of a bunker, half in sand, half in grass.

If you face such a lie, use a lofted wedge and lay the clubface wide open at address.

Swing back the same way you would on a normal bunker shot.

Swing the club down more briskly than normal, contacting a spot about one or two inches behind the ball. Make sure to hit harder than you usually do.

When facing this lie, use a lofted wedge and make your normal sand-play swing.

DIFFERENT STROKES FOR DIFFERENT FOLKS

The type of swing a player employs, its speed, the texture of the sand, and the degree of bounce built into his or her sand wedge all determine how far behind the ball the club should enter the sand. Some players do better hitting two inches behind the ball. Some of you will achieve better results hitting four inches behind the ball, as did the great Claude Harmon.

The bottom line: When in doubt, hit three inches behind the ball. (Exception: When the sand is wet, hit one inch behind the ball.)

In playing sand shots, when in doubt hit three inches behind the ball.

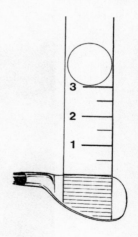

You'll be penalized if you hit the sand while taking a practice swing in a greenside bunker. Therefore, it's best to rehearse your swing outside the bunker.

Swing at a spot in the grass about two to four inches behind an imaginary ball, just as you plan to do in the bunker.

Practicing your swing outside the bunker is the smart thing to do.

DON'T ALWAYS BLAST THE BALL OUT OF SAND

If the lip of a bunker is low, the lie is clean, and you have plenty of green to work with, go ahead and chip, rather than playing a normal blast or "explosion" shot.

Play the ball back in your stance with your hands ahead of it.

Make a wristless backswing.

Swing your arms through using a smooth, flowing action.

Sometimes, in sand, a chip is a good shot to play.

When the ball is partially buried in an upslope near the front lip of a bunker and you face a shot to a tight pin placement, do what Chi Chi Rodriguez does:

Set up with the toe of your putter aimed at a spot just behind the ball.

Pick the club almost straight up.

Pull the club down sharply, so the toe digs down into the sand.

The ball will pop out and fly in a slight left-to-right pattern, so aim slightly left of the hole when assuming your address position. It's an amazing trick shot that really works!

A putter can help you recover from a difficult lie like this one.

TAKE A LESSON FROM GARY PLAYER

The greatest sand players of all time, Seve Ballesteros, Julius Boros, Chi Chi Rodriguez, and Claude Harmon, were not born with supertalent. They became proficient in sand because they practiced hard.

No one practiced as hard as Gary Player. As a youngster, he never left the practice area until he had holed five bunker shots. And today, he still practices diligently.

It is not necessarily true that "practice makes perfect." But it does help, as Player and other greats have proved. One two-hour session will probably do wonders for your bunker game.

Practice may not make perfect, but it will help you play better sand shots.

DOWN AND DIRTY

When the ball is buried below the surface of the sand, let this be a signal to make an upright swing and hit down sharply.

To hit this shot, use a pitching wedge, or be sure to close the clubface of a sand wedge to help you get under the ball. Also, be sure to contact a spot in the sand, about one inch behind the ball.

If your lie looks like this, make a steep back-swing and hit down sharply.

HOW TO PLAY A LONG BUNKER SHOT FROM A GOOD LIE

Here's a setup secret that will help you play a 30-to-40-yard bunker shot from a good lie in sand: Assume a closed stance, placing your right foot farther from the target line than your left.

This address position promotes the shallow inside-inside swing path that's needed to send the ball flying on a low trajectory, toward the hole. It also helps you take a shallow cut of sand.

On long bunker shots, a closed stance will promote the proper swing path.

STAY DOWN

Golfers who top sand shots usually come out of their flexed position before impact. Therefore, the club hits the top of the ball instead of digging into the sand.

If topping shots is your problem, maintain the bend in your waist and knees, and keep your eyes focused on a spot behind the ball until after impact.

To avoid top shots,
maintain the flex in your knees and the bend
in your waist until after impact.

UP AGAINST THE WALL

When the ball is very close to the back wall of a bunker, don't think you always have to hit out sideways. You can go for the flag, provided you remember to choke down on the club, set the clubface wide open, swing the club almost straight up in the air on the backswing, and swing down, making sure to keep the clubface open.

A very steep backswing is a technical must when playing a shot that's close to the back wall of a bunker.

CURE FOR A "CHUNK"

If you dig the club down too deeply into the sand and "chunk" the ball a short distance, here's a cure:

Think about finishing with your chest pointing slightly left of the hole. This will encourage you to uncoil your upper body and, in turn, swing the club nicely through the sand with your arms.

*Striving for a good finish
can help you make a good swing.*

TAKE YOUR PICK

When testing various sand wedges, buy the one that gives you the strongest degree of confidence when you look at it, and test it by hitting bunker shots. Be sure, too, to buy a sand wedge that features the right bounce (flange) for the type of sand you normally hit out of.

The best sand wedge for you is the one that looks good to the eye and works well when you test it.

HOW TO PLAY
A LONG BUNKER SHOT
FROM A BAD LIE

When the ball is buried in a bunker and you face a 30-to-40-yard shot, select a pitching wedge and follow these instructions:

Set the clubface square to the target.

Make a very upright backswing.

Pull the club down into a spot about a half-inch behind the ball.

In this situation, the club should contact a spot a half-inch behind the ball.

½ in

ESTABLISH FIRM FOOTING

To enhance your balance and encourage a fluid swing of the arms when playing bunker shots, be sure to wriggle your feet into the sand.

Setting your feet down slightly in the sand also helps you test the texture and depth of the bunker, without violating *The Rules of Golf*. This testing process will help you hit a better shot.

Think "feet first" when setting up to play a bunker shot.

AIMING AID

To help you hit a precise area in the sand, between two and four inches behind the ball, set up with the clubhead raised in the air and aimed at that area. Don't keep the leading edge too close to the ball. Don't keep the club too close to the sand, either; you'll be penalized two strokes if it touches the sand before impact.

In setting up to play a bunker shot,
set the club above your ultimate contact
area, in the sand.

THE "FRIED-EGG" LIE
RECOVERY SHOT

In the course of a round, you might confront a fried-egg lie. You'll know you're faced with this if the ball looks like an egg yolk surrounded by the "white" sand.

To handle this lie, open your stance, close the clubface slightly, and concentrate on removing the entire egg.

Dig out the entire "egg"
when playing from a fried-egg lie.

SPLIT YOUR GRIP

In order to get a good feel for how the wrists hinge early in the backswing, while swinging on an upright plane, and while slapping the sand with the club, separate your hands when gripping. This "split-grip" hold will allow you to experience the hinge of the wrists.

This split-grip hold will help you learn proper sand-play technique.

THE RIGHT SAND WEDGE FOR SOFT SAND

If the sand at the course you play is soft and heavy, carry a sand wedge that features a generous degree of "bounce."

Bounce means the degree to which the rear edge of the club-head's flange lies below its leading edge, when the clubhead is held in a perfectly vertical position. The sand wedge is the only club in your bag with this amount of bounce feature built into the flange. The correct amount of bounce should be 10 to 15 degrees of angle on the flange.

This type of club will allow you to take a shallow cut of sand.

In soft sand, a sand wedge featuring a generous bounce works best.

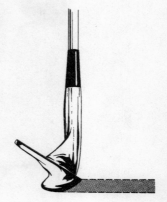

If you have trouble swinging through the sand and reaching the hole, ask your pro the following questions about your sand wedge:

Does it have enough bounce for the sand at your home course? Does it have a wide enough flange? Does it feature approximately 56 degrees of loft? If the answers to these questions is no, buy a new sand wedge.

Next, make sure you don't open the clubface quite so much. Keep it fairly square, and focus your attention on swinging all the way through to the finish. Visualize a quick move through the sand.

If you're having trouble in sand, buy a sand wedge with the correct loft and bounce.

SUPERCONTROL

If you hit short bunker shots too far past the hole, you could be swinging too fast and not taking enough sand. Streamline your swing by stopping at the three-quarter point. Then concentrate on throwing the club down into the sand and employing a short finish.

This shorter action will promote a smoother swing, especially in the finish, thereby allowing you to hit soft-landing shots.

Shorten your backswing to hit the short sand shot.

If the sand at your course is firm, use a sand wedge that features very little bounce.

This club-selection strategy will apply to wet sand as well. You may even need to use the pitching wedge in these situations.

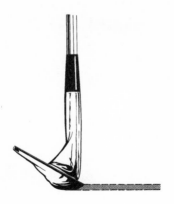

*A sand wedge with a narrow flange and
little bounce works best in firm sand.*

CAN YOU DIG IT?

To help you make a more upright swing and dig down into firm sand, assume a narrow stance. The narrow stance will keep you centered, and encourage a V-shaped swinging action.

*Assuming a narrow stance will help you hit
down into the sand.*

X MARKS THE SPOT

When playing bunker shots, it's important to take you
off the ball. You must concentrate on a spot in the sand
two to four inches behind the ball. That's where the club should
make contact. Here's how to train yourself to hit the sand, not
the ball:

Draw an X in the sand, between two inches and four inches
behind the ball. Swing back, then down, removing the X. After
just a few swings, you'll see how simple it is to hit good sand
shots.

*To be a better sand player, practice
removing an X you've drawn behind the
ball.*

WHEN TO STRENGTHEN YOUR GRIP

If you hit extra-low sand shots that hit the bunker wall and roll back down into the bunker, try assuming a stronger grip.

This grip, combined with an open clubface, will help you slide the club under the ball more easily.

To check that you're holding the club correctly, look down and confirm that the V's formed by the thumbs and forefingers of each hand point toward your right shoulder.

A strong grip will help you hit higher sand shots.

STRAIGHT DOWN
THE MIDDLE

If you have trouble maintaining a firm hold on the club and keeping the clubface open through impact, point your left thumb straight down the middle of the grip and lying flat against it.

*When gripping, straighten your left thumb
to enhance your control of the club
in the hit zone.*

DOWN UNDER

To hit a good shot out of relatively firm-based sand, square the clubface at address, stay behind the ball through impact, and hit more down and under the ball.

*In firm sand, stay down longer
through impact.*

THE ONE AND ONLY

If you forget everything else about playing sand shots, remember this one tip:

   The idea is to cut out a strip of sand from the bunker, upon which the ball sits. Don't even think about the ball. Simply pick out an area between two and four inches behind the ball, then take out that area with the club. The rest, as they say, is history.

On bunker shots, don't hit the ball.
Cut out a wide area of sand,
behind the ball and past it.

CHOKE DOWN
FOR CONTROL

To help you hit a more delicate short sand shot, choke down a few inches on the club. This setup adjustment will allow you to swing the club faster without hitting the ball too far.

*Choking down will enhance your touch
on short sand shots.*

THE LOWDOWN
ON LOW SHOTS

If your problem is hitting sand shots too low, you're probably assuming an exaggerated closed stance, plus playing the ball too far back in your stance.

To remedy this problem, aim your feet slightly left of target, in an open position, and play the ball off your left heel.

*Play the ball off your left heel, in an open
stance, to hit higher sand shots.*

SLAP HAPPY

On almost all sand shots, you want the feel of slapping the sand with the club through impact. To promote this action and hit a soft floating shot, unhinge your wrists and release your hands early in the downswing.

*To promote this type of sand shot, practice
an early release action.*

To play a left-to-right cut shot that flies over the lip of a bunker and lands softly, set up open, make a compact upright swing, then swing across the ball through impact.

This technique is ideal for super-short sand shots, or when the green slopes away from you.

To impart cut spin on the ball, swing through across the target line.

CHAPTER 3

HOW TO CHIP LIKE A PRO

STOP THE "TOP"

Topping chip shots is a common fault among amateur golfers. The usual cause is straightening your legs just before impact. When you rise up, the club rises up, too, so you hit the ball with the bottom of the clubface rather than its sweet spot.

To help you hit solid chips, flex your knees at address, then maintain that flex from the start of the swing to its finish.

*Maintain your knee flex to prevent hitting
the dreaded top shot.*

LOOK AT THE LIE

When you hit any chip shot, carefully survey the lie.

Ask yourself whether the ball will fly extra fast off the club-face owing to blades of grass becoming trapped between the clubface and the ball at impact. If the ball is sitting in relatively high fringe grass, that's probably what will happen. Counter this, and encourage soft flight, by taking a more lofted club—namely, the sand wedge or lofted wedge—rather than a pitching wedge.

*To hit a chip from this type of lie, use a
more lofted club.*

REHEARSE YOUR CHIP STROKE BEFORE YOU HIT THE BALL

Before addressing the ball, take a couple of practice swings to feel the correct length and firmness of stroke that's needed to chip the ball close to the cup. Remember, every chip is slightly different; it takes precision to hit each shot the correct distance. Of all the shots in golf, the practice swings for these shots are most important.

Don't rush; take a couple of practice swings to rehearse the correct technique.

ON THE SPOT

Many high handicappers hit fairly straight chip shots that roll well by the hole. That's because they concentrate too hard on the hole. If this is your problem, here's how to solve it:

Pick a spot or circle on the green to land the ball. Concentrate on that spot. Pick the club that will allow you to loft the ball to that spot. Swing. The ball will hit the spot and run to the hole like a putt.

TAILORING THE TIP: If you face a 30-foot chip and you want to play a pitching wedge, remember your chipping calculus. The ideal shot should fly 15 feet, hit the spot, then roll the remaining 15 feet. Half in the air, half on the ground.

Spot chipping will enhance your distance control.

WHEN YOU HINGE
YOUR WRISTS

When playing a very delicate chip off a tight lie, incorporate some wrist action into your backswing. This enhances your feel and helps you nip the ball off the manicured fringe grass.

*When chipping off tightly mowed fringe, let
your wrists hinge slightly on the backswing.*

SNUGGLE UP

Standing too far away from the ball is one reason many high handicappers mishit chip shots. Learn from their errors.

In setting up, allow your right arm to bend slightly at the elbow. This will help you snuggle up to the ball (without crowding it) and hit clean, crisp chip shots.

A comfortably correct setup is critical to hitting good chip shots.

LONG CHIPS: THE RIGHT CLUB AND THE RIGHT TECHNIQUE

When playing a very long running chip, either play a pitching wedge, with the ball well back in your stance, or use a low-lofted club.

For the low running wedge, keep the hands and wrists quiet; concentrate on swinging the club back and through with your arms. Be sure to lean the clubshaft toward the target, then keep the hands leading into impact.

On long chips, concentrate on swinging the club with your arms.

KNOW WHAT YOUR CLUBS CAN DO

To develop expert hand-eye coordination and enhance your touch around the greens, practice chip shots using different wedges and varying the clubface angle, until you learn how far the ball flies in the air, and rolls on the green, with each. Your wedges can be used in many ways to hit an array of specialty shots.

To enhance your touch, practice hitting chips with different wedges and adjusting the clubface angle.

THANKS, CLAUDE

Claude Harmon, the 1948 Master's winner, had a reputation as one of the finest short-game players—and instuctors—of all time.

Harmon believed that to hit solid, on-target chips consistently, it was essential that the follow-through of the chip swing be short.

To help a student groove the correct hit-and-resist type of follow-through action, he would hold a club at a 45-degree angle, in the manner shown in the photograph, then tell the player to swing.

When the student hit through the ball, the shaft of his club would inevitably strike the standing shaft, giving an immediate sensation of resistance.

If you practice this drill with the help of a friend, you can't help but learn how to groove the proper short follow-through action.

Practice hitting the shaft to groove the correct follow-through action.

TRY A NEW GRIP

To help hit more accurate short chip shots, try draping your left forefinger over the first three fingers of your right hand, as many tour pros do.

This grip is normally used for putting, but it can help you guide your chips along a line to the hole.

*This unique putting grip can help you
hit straighter chip shots.*

V FOR VICTORY

The great Johnny Revolta used to tell his students that if they concentrated on swinging the V shape, formed by the arms, using a short brisk motion, their chipping skills would quickly improve to expert level.

Follow this advice, and make sure to let your wrists hinge ever so slightly in the takeaway while keeping them rock solid on the downswing. By the time the clubhead reaches the ball, the wrists should be firm and the V secure. Maintain the V through to the finish.

Swing the V shape, formed by your arms, to improve your chipping skills.

TREVINO OBSERVATION

To be a master chipper, like Lee Trevino, try the swing action he uses. Swing the clubhead straight back along the target line or slightly outside it. At the completion of your takeaway, bring your hands more toward your body so that the club swings to inside, making a sort of mini-loop.

If you do this correctly, the sole of the clubhead, not its leading edge, will ultimately hit the ground at impact. Not only will this action prevent a "chili dip," it will promote clean, crisp clubface-to-ball contact, and the straightest possible roll.

If you swing back like Lee Trevino, the sole of the club will hit the ground.

HOW TO GROOVE A WRISTLESS CHIP STROKE

If you pick the club straight up in the air at the start of the backswing and mishit chips, this drill will help tame your hands and wrists:

Address a ball that's positioned back in your stance.

Have a friend place a second ball along the target line, a few inches beyond your right foot.

Now swing back, sweeping the second ball away.

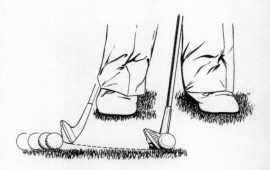

This drill will help you groove a wristless chip stroke.

If you feel that you just can't swing the club through freely on the downswing, and your chip shots fly off-line, you're probably swinging the club back much too far inside the target line. From this position, it's virtually impossible to square the clubface to the ball at impact.

To help you groove a straighter backswing path, first build a practice station by laying two medium irons down on the ground, side by side, about 12 inches apart.

Place a ball on the ground, midway between them. Address the ball.

Make your takeaway action. If the clubhead hits the clubshaft closest to you or crosses it, your backswing path is too flat. Correct this problem by practicing your takeaway over and over, until you keep the clubhead inside the trough.

To correct an overly flat backswing path, swing inside a homemade trough.

If your ball is sitting in wiry greenside rough and the pin is cut near the edge of the green closest to you, do what PGA Tour professional Bob Gilder does to hit a superb recovery shot.

In setting up, play the ball off your left heel and aim your body left of the target line.

Choke far down on the club. Keep the club open and square to the target.

Swing the club back outside the target line, then across the ball coming through, keeping the clubface open. Keep the follow-through short.

Choke down on the club and set up open when recovering from wiry rough.

THE BARE FACTS

For some reason, average golfers seem to use a seven iron for all chip shots. The pros, on the other hand, use different clubs to handle different lies. So should you.

When chipping off a bare lie, where grass is sparse, play a lofted wedge.

This club makes it easier to loft the ball into the air. If you're worried about hitting the ball so high that it stops too quickly, play the ball back in your stance with your hands ahead of it. This setup will cause you to come into impact more sharply, and the club's effective loft will be reduced. Therefore, you'll get all the roll you need to reach the hole.

When the grass is sparse, chip with a lofted wedge.

THE NO–SPIN CHIP

One great way to hit supersoft, superaccurate chips from short distances is to employ the "bent-arms" swing method made popular by Paul Runyan.

Here's how:

Take your normal chipping address, but keep your elbows widely separated.

Keeping your hands and lower body quiet, rock your shoulders and upper body back and through, as if rocking a baby.

Feel how rhythmically the club swings, almost as if it were a pendulum. Watch how the ball seems to "hunt" the hole.

Assume this setup position to chip the Paul Runyan way.

A very common swing fault made by the average club golfer when hitting long chip shots is using too much knee action. Keep your knees "frozen" until the precise moment of impact.

This will allow your hands and arms to correctly dominate the chipping stroke, and enhance your distance and direction control.

The player: just before the moment of impact, when the knees will release.

PLAY BALL

High handicappers tend to pull chip shots because they play the ball too far forward in their stance. Setting up this way causes you to set your hands behind the ball and, in turn, aim the clubface left of target.

To remedy this direction problem, play the ball in the center of your stance or close behind it.

*If you hit pull shots playing the ball
in this position, move it back into the center
of your stance.*

HIT THROUGH, NOT "AT" THE BALL

To chip like a pro, don't scoop the ball. Swing the club down through the ball, toward the hole. Make sure you brush the grass after contacting the ball.

When chipping off fringe grass, swing the club through the ball, then toward the hole.

HOW TO STOP HITTING BEHIND THE BALL

When you hit behind the ball you hit a "fat" shot, meaning that the ball flies only a very short distance, landing well shy of the hole.

This shot can be traced to an overly loose grip. The loose grip can cause you to throw, or flip, the club down into the turf behind the ball.

Hold the club more firmly, with a pressure of about six on the Jim McLean grip-scale of 1–10 ("one" is super-light, "five" is medium-pressure, "ten" is super-tight). Then maintain this firm grip pressure throughout the stroke.

If you hit fat chip shots, try gripping the club more firmly.

WHAT CLUB TO CHOOSE WHEN CHIPPING OFF A SEVERE UPHILL LIE

If you face a chip off a severe uphill lie and you think the correct club is a sand wedge, play a pitching wedge instead. The reason: When you swing through along the steep incline, the effective loft of the club is increased; i.e., the pitching wedge acts like a sand wedge.

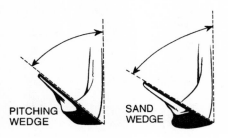

PITCHING WEDGE   SAND WEDGE

Off a severe uphill lie, play a less lofted pitching wedge (left) instead of a more lofted sand wedge (right).

STEADY NOW

If you watch the best chippers on the PGA Tour, you'll notice that they keep their heads perfectly still throughout the backswing. This prevents them from swaying off the ball and ultimately hitting a bad shot.

To prevent swaying, keep your head perfectly still on the backswing.

WHEN TO USE WRIST ACTION

When the ball is sitting down slightly, in a bad lie in the fringe, allow your right wrist to hinge on the backswing.

This wrist action will promote a slightly steeper backswing and let you hit crisply down into the ball.

Off bad lies, allow your right wrist to hinge slightly on the backswing.

WHAT CLUB TO CHOOSE WHEN CHIPPING OFF A SEVERE DOWNHILL LIE

If you face a chip off a severe downhill lie and you think the correct club is a pitching wedge, play a sand wedge instead. The reason: When you swing through along the downhill slope the effective loft of the the club will be decreased; i.e., the sand wedge will act like a pitching wedge.

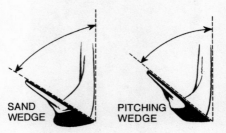

SAND WEDGE

PITCHING WEDGE

*Off a severe downhill lie, play a sand wedge
(left) instead of a pitching wedge (right).*

ACCURACY KEY

When chipping, don't ever let the clubhead get ahead hands on the downswing; let the hands lead the clubhead.

To promote the proper action, let your left forearm and left wrist pull the club through the shot.

*To hit pro-type chip shots, let your hands
play the lead role on the downswing.*

PRACTICE TIP

To enhance your chipping touch, practice hitting to various targets.

Drop six balls down on the fringe, then chip each one to a different location.

Repeat the drill several times.

If you want to save par from the fringe on the course, practice chip shots of different lengths.

BALL–POSITION STRATEGY WHEN THE GREEN SLOPES FROM RIGHT TO LEFT

When hitting to a green that slopes rather severely from right to left, play the ball closer to your right foot. This position will help you keep the ball on the "high" side of the hole, and prevent a pull.

Play the ball back in your stance when hitting to a right-to-left sloping green.

THE BUMP

When there's a steep bank between you and a hole cut close to the edge of the green, select a pitching wedge.

Play the ball back in your stance with your hands well ahead of it.

Lean about 70 percent of your weight on the left foot.

Keep the club moving low through impact.

The higher the grass, the farther you will have to fly the ball. Don't worry; the mound will kill the momentum of the shot. The ball should bounce once or twice, hit the green, then trickle to the hole.

In this situation, play the bump shot.

Good chippers know how the ball will perform in the air and on the ground with all their wedges. So should you.

Go to the practice green, or out on the course, and hit shots with all three wedges, using consistent ball and clubface positions. For example, if you play the ball off your left heel with the pitching wedge, and keep the clubface square, do the same with the other clubs. Note how the ball reacts. Once you record the results in your brain, vary the ball and clubface positions and see what happens.

To become an expert chipper, practice hitting shots with the pitching wedge, sand wedge, and lofted wedge.

DON'T LIFT
YOUR LEFT FOOT

To prevent an overly long, overly steep chipping swing, keep your left foot planted on the ground during the backswing. Lifting your left heel high off the ground can cause you to pick the club straight up into the air, then chop down on it going through.

To hit good chip shots, keep your left foot planted on the ground.

BALL–POSITION STRATEGY
WHEN THE GREEN SLOPES
FROM LEFT TO RIGHT

When hitting to a green that slopes rather severely from left to right, play the ball closer to your left foot. This position will help you keep the ball on the "high" side of the hole, and prevent a push.

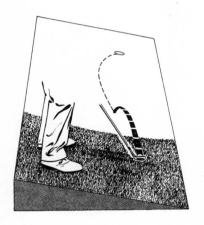

When preparing to hit a left-to-right chip,
play the ball closer to your front foot.

ONE–HANDED STROKE

To enhance your feel for playing chips, practice hitting shots with your right hand only.

You'll be amazed how well your chips will work if you do the following:

1. Allow the right wrist to cock in the takeaway;

2. Maintain the same angle of the right wrist through impact;

3. Swing the club smoothly, back and through;

4. Never "slap" at the ball with the right hand, or allow the right wrist to flatten out.

Practice hitting right-hand chips to enhance your feel and direction control.

ABOUT THE AUTHORS

JIM MCLEAN is the Director of Instruction for KSL Properties' Doral Golf Resort and Spa in Miami, Florida, and PGA West/La Quinta in Palm Springs, California. Chosen 1994 PGA Teacher of the Year, Jim has instructed many of the top PGA Tour pros, including 1992 U.S. Open winner Tom Kite, Brad Faxon, and Peter Jacobsen. He is a Master Teaching Professional at *GOLF Magazine* and golf instructor for the Academy of Golf on The Golf Channel. He is also the Director of Instruction for the Chelsea Piers Golf Facility in Manhattan, New York.

McLean has written numerous best-selling instructional books, including *The Eight-Step Swing* and *The Putter's Pocket Companion*, and produced the highly successful videos *The X Factor* and *20 Problems/20 Solutions*. He has also lectured for the U.S. military and conducts numerous instructional seminars for the PGA. He resides with his family in Miami, and owns and operates the Jim McLean Golf Schools, headquartered at the Doral Golf Resort and Spa.

JOHN ANDRISANI is the senior editor of instruction at *GOLF Magazine*. He is also the co-author of several books, including *Natural Golf*, with Seve Ballesteros, *101 Supershots*, with Chi Chi Rodriguez, *Grip It and Rip It!* with John Daly, and *The Golf Doctor*, with Robin McMillan.

A fine player in his own right, Andrisani is a former course record holder and a former winner of the American Golf Writers' Championship.

JEFF BLANTON is a Florida-based photographer whose work has appeared in *GOLF Magazine*.

KEN LEWIS is a British artist who is recogized as one of the leading illustrators of the golf swing.

WEDGE GAME NOTES

WEDGE GAME NOTES